LARN YARSELF
NORFOLK

"I should like true Norfolk to survive because of its expressive vocabulary and vivid turn of phrase - so much more vigorous (and honest) than the gobbledegook of the bureaucrats and sociologists, with which we are nowadays so smothered that the language itself is in danger of losing its meaning. The English country dialects, if they do indeed remain alive, may well become the last repository - outside of old books - of good plain English."

Jonathan Mardle (Broad Norfolk) 1973.

Cover picture: The Smithy at New Buckenham, Mr. A. G. Reeve, blacksmith, pauses to mardle with his friends, Mr. C. Goodman and Mr. D. Filley. First published in the EDP in 1950. From the collection of Neil Storey and reproduced with kind permission.

Larn Yarself NORFOLK

Keith Skipper

NOSTALGIA *Publications*

TOFTWOOD • DEREHAM • NORFOLK

Originally Published by:
NOSTALGIA PUBLICATIONS

First Impressions: 1996
Reprinted: 1996, 1998, 1999

Reprinted Sept 2000 and Jan 2002 by.
JOHN NICKALLS
Oak Farm Bungalow, Suton,
Wymondham, Norfolk NR18 9SH

© Nostalgia Publications 1996

ISBN 0 947630 13 9

Design and Typesetting:
NOSTALGIA PUBLICATIONS

Printed by:
BARNWELL'S PRINT LTD.
Aylsham, Norfolk NR11 6ET

Contents

Acknowledgements 6

Introduction 7

The First Test 9

SECTION ONE - Lessons and Exercises 11

   Lesson One - Beware False Images! 13

   Lesson One Exercises 16

   Lesson Two - Accept The Impossible! 17

   Lesson Two Exercises 20

   Lesson Three - Ignore The Rumours! 21

   Lesson Three Exercises 26

   Lesson Four - Mind The Double Negative 27

   Lesson Four Exercises 30

   Lesson Five - Now Put It All Together! ... 31

   Lesson Five Exercises 34

SECTION TWO - Norfolk Stories and Verses .. 35

   There It Is! 37

   Colourful Words 38

   Norfolk Dumplin's Recipe 40

   A Good View 41

   It's A Pushover 42

   Hay Hay! 44

   Preaching The Word 45

   Lazy Wind 46

SECTION THREE - A Norfolk Dictionary 47

   A Norfolk Dictionary 49

   The Final Exam 94

Acknowledgements

I suppose most of the furrows had been ploughed by the time I reached the headlands. But I am proud to cultivate the rich dialect soil with this new guide to its unfading beauty.

Warmest thanks to publisher Terry Davy for his practical expertise and unstinting support. Artist friend Ken Walton has provided splendid illustrations to show how a sensitive Yorkshireman can aid one of Norfolk's main cultural causes.

I am grateful to the Eastern Daily Press for permission to reproduce details of their impressive dialect survey of 1993 – a survey designed to confirm our vernacular does have a secure future.

Salutes also for all moving spirits behind other dialect offerings included to underline its resilience and charm. Special thanks to John Kett for his cheerful support with the dictionary.

My customary bouquet for wife Diane who enjoyed her crash course in "larnin' Norfolk" as she headed for the word processor. Cor, blarst, she's wholly ewseful!

Keith Skipper
Cromer 1996

Introduction

"To poke fun at a Norfolk man's speech and customs is an amusement of no recent birth. Some five centuries since, a Monk of Peterborough wrote his 'Descriptio Norfolciensium', wherein his pictures of our old peasant life are ludicrously portrayed; in short, it is obvious throughout that our monastic author forgot to confine himself to the truth."

So complained Walton N. Dew when he served up "A Dyshe of Norfolk Dumplings" in 1898. Precisely the same sentiments remain in full circulation as cheap laughs and ignorance mock efforts to present the Norfolk dialect and mannerisms in an honest way.

This is but the latest in a long line of exercises designed to help the cause, to shed a little light on a precious corner where cobwebs of indifference can too easily multiply alongside the dust of derision.

If Norfolk wants to maintain a reputation for dewin' diffrunt it must be heard taking delight in an essential strand of that alternative pattern. "Use it or lose it" can apply just as much to the vernacular as to the village shop or pub.

A comprehensive glossary of words and expressions is accompanied by stories, verses, illustrations, handy lessons and little tests. These have been carefully selected to show the full range of uses to which dialect can be put as well as the strength of support it has received - and is still receiving - from some enlightened quarters.

The difficulties are not underplayed. Remember as your frustrations mount that the Norfolk dialect is purely oral in origin. Some claim the Norfolk tongue is virtually beyond writing down. Most agree that only natives can speak it with any degree of comfort.

But there has to be general approval for the fight to retain something supposed to be on its last legs well over a century ago. Back to Walter N. Dew for an inspiring text as the battle continues:

"Never be ashamed of the dialect and customs of good old Norfolk. If we are behind the times, compared with other counties, we can console ourselves with the thought that Norfolk men have played their part, and that right well, in the stirring events of our national history."

Keith Skipper

The First Test

The traditional way of finding out if a person comes from Norfolk is to pose a question which was used as a test during the 1914-18 War:

A Norfolk nurse, thinking she recognised a wounded soldier as coming from her own home village, whispered in his ear: "Ha' yer fa'r got a dickey, bor?". He knew it meant "Has your father got a donkey, boy?" and mumbled through his bandages: "Yis, an' he want a fule ter roide 'im, will yew cum?". That means: "Yes, and he wants a fool to ride him, will you come?".

Norfolk people, on meeting in faraway places, still tend to use that question and answer as recognition signals. And the usual follow-up is "All the way ter Swoffum ter dew a day's troshin' fer noffin' - thass suffin'!" in an exaggerated drawl to caricature their own dialect.

Of course, some would say you can always tell a Norfolk man - but you can't tell him much!

Section One

Lessons and
Exercises

GRAVE COUGH

An old woman with a rasping cough was walking through the village churchyard.

"Oh dear, yew'll hatter git rid o' that rotten corff" said a passer-by.

"Dunt want ter git rid onnit."

"Dunt yer?"

"No - there's pletty a' layin' bowt here what'd be wholly glad onnit!"

Lesson One - Beware False Images!

Ask a stranger for a pen picture of Norfolk, and chances are you will get a mixture of plump turkeys, The Singing Postman, mustard and sugar-beet.

Every region is forced to suffer an overdose of stereotyped images. All Welshmen wear pit helmets and sing. Scots don't go out on a flag day. The Irish have to be retrained after a tea-break. Yorkshiremen are too arrogant to make mistakes. Londoners treat everyone else as inferiors ...

We shake our pitchforks and then smile at such generalisations, many of them peddled by television "personalities" from the Mummerzet Charm School or comedians looking for the quickest punchline below the belt.

Norfolk's comparative isolation has its virtues, even if traditional caution is still too often mistaken for calculated coldness. Being on the road to nowhere invites accusations of being out of touch, though those pointing accusing fingers regularly fail to disguise their envy.

The growing numbers of the worldly and the well-heeled seeking sanctuary in rural retreats simply underline the ambivalent attitude towards places like Norfolk. Nice spot - shame about the peasants!

Norfolk's customary response is to make full use of that wholly predictable guarded reaction to challenge and change, stamping a delightful brand of understatement on so many humorous yarns.

Perhaps the "friendly invasion" of Americans during the last war left a bigger mark than had been generally recognised. In any event, it proved a useful rehearsal for good-natured bouts to come between hard-boiled natives and newcomers with the missionary zeal.

Where Norfolk takes genuine umbrage is where the whole business descends into bucolic buffoonery. So many drama productions on television and radio - and occasionally on stage - make a real mockery of geography, local pride and artistic accuracy.

Norfolk, it seems, is a little place wedged somewhere between Devon and Dorset. The locals mutter "oooh-aaarrr! oooh-aaarrr!" roughly along the same lines as other stage rustics with vacant faces, plodding walks and the guarantee of a role in the next epic needing that authentic country feel.

Embarrassed mutterings about the accent being so hard to imitate do nothing to remove the sting from insults to both Norfolk and the West Country. Matters are made worse by high-profile national advertising campaigns littered with country bumpkins using invented words like "smuckerlin'", "broidle" and "scruttles".

Recent commercials for sauces starred a lusty hayseed called Jed and two likely lasses referred to as Norfolk broads. Sussex-based Van den Bergh Foods, which own Norwich-based Colman's, said the accent and made-up words were chosen to "reflect the heartiness, warmth and Norwich origins of the brand."

Locals who had the audacity to find the commercials insulting were called bad sports. "Here we are helping to create new jobs and prosperity - and we get this sort of ingratitude!" is the stock response from metropolitan advertising agencies working on the principle that to get something wrong is the easiest way to make an impact.

Of course, Norfolk isn't the only county to be exploited in this way. The "yokel" bandwagon keeps on coming over the brow of the hill in the name of commerce - and that's supposed to make it acceptable from Downham to Dartmoor. There was another predictable outcry when the "Smuckerlin' Good" campaign was used to promote Norfolk as a holiday destination. The High Sheriff of Norfolk, John Birkbeck, led a fresh chorus of disapproval: "It is so vulgar. I feel we are being so belittled and made fools of; there are lots of sound Norfolk words which can be used". Wholly right, ole partner!

To lump all country dialects together in one big rustic pot is a wicked affront to so many areas rich with individual character and respect for truly local tradition. After all, those very qualities attracted most holidaymakers and settlers in the first place.

While there can be no hard-and-fast rules for local dialects, there are some generally acceptable principles to follow. For example, the vast majority of Norfolk people salute a "bew'ful" day as the sun beats down. Yet one of the county's leading businessmen - indeed, he is an international figure - sends his products to all parts with the label "bootiful" round their necks.

His lorries trumpet the wrong sound! The first syllable of the adjective rhymes with "new" and the "t" is almost inaudible. Bernard Matthews is accepted as the archetypal Norfolkman as he sings his turkeys' praises in television commercials across the nation. While he insists on "bootiful", and inspires a few more thousand bad impressions, Norfolk's cry of "gobbledegook!" will continue.

So, the search for the genuine article - or as close to it as possible - is the first important lesson on any dialect syllabus. To accept mutilation and mockery as inevitable by-products of a modern age, a smaller world, is to blatantly renounce the spirit of a people and a place.

Lesson One Exercises

✧ Think of some less predictable images of Norfolk as you prepare your own pen picture of the county – e.g. big skies, round-towered churches, fluffy dumplings and flint-knapping.

✧ Do the same for other counties and regions and rid yourself of preconceived notions. Try to see Dorset without cider, Yorkshire minus cricket and the Cotswolds stripped of antique shops.

Lesson Two - Accept The Impossible!

I have mentioned already that there are no set rules for writing down dialect. That is why so many outstanding supporters have called it "mission impossible" - only to make stirring attempts to prove themselves wrong!

Dick Bagnall-Oakeley, Norfolk dialect expert, naturalist and teacher at Gresham's School in Holt, led the field in recent years despite all his own misgivings about committing the local language to paper.

"Its accents and vowel sounds are too subtle, too varied and too rich for the alphabet which suffices for the rest of the English tongue.

"Sometimes you will see somebody making an attempt at the impossible - written Norfolk - the capture of broad Norfolk in an alphabet of a mere 26 letters."

These difficulties had been underlined in 1930 by Russell Colman in his foreword to B. Knyvet Wilson's "Norfolk Tales and Memories". Mr Colman, Lord Lieutenant of the county, had never experienced any trouble in speaking Norfolk, "but, quite frankly, I do not know how to write it".

"If I have not forgotten my schoolboy lessons there are five vowels, and sometimes two extra. For 'Norfolk' that does not appear to be anything like what I require.

"Take the following sentence and render it into 'Norfolk':-

There's nothing ever goes down that old driftway unless it be a farm-cart.

There's *northen* ever *go* down that *ood* driftway *doo* that's only a *farm-cart*.

"Now in all the five words I have italicised

I want a fresh supply of vowels, and unless I may have them I can't write 'Norfolk'".

It didn't stop him having a go, and countless others have followed despite the obvious problems of spelling, a limited vocabulary and being confronted with the question of how to indicate intonation.

The picture can be complicated further by two "confessions" - that dialect can vary considerably from one part of the county to another, and certain words have been the subject of unjustified regional claims.

Walter Rye, who wrote prolifically on his adopted county, said in the preamble to his "Glossary of East Anglia" in 1895:- "If it were possible to divide the words into districts, we should no doubt find a great difference between the dialect of one part of a county from that of another. 'When I left Strumpshaw for Ryburgh,' said my old skipper Tungate, a very careful observer, 'the words fared very strange to me'."

That observation still holds good - the fishermen of Sheringham and Cromer have a different sound to their counterparts at

---

DRY RESPONSE

In the early days of the Second World War, two Norfolk labourers were pulling sugar beet on a large open field in the pouring rain. One of them had happened to see a newspaper that morning and said to the other: "I see in the EDP th'ole Jarmans hev gone inter Warsaw". The other pulled up his coat collar a little higher, gazed at the brooding skies and remarked: "Well, they hent got much of a day for't, hev they?" - and went on with his job without another word.

Yarmouth and Gorleston - and there are examples of words and expressions being peculiar to a particular village or even to just one family.

My mother called me a "want" - rhyming with "pant" - when I had done something silly or wrong (she had plenty of practice!). Extensive inquiries have failed to reveal either the derivation of the word or anyone else thus described for mild misdemeanours.

Norfolk should remain wary of staking sole claims on certain words. It is the intonation which varies and gives it a distinctive local flavour.

"Tizzick", a troublesome cough, is still used regularly in this county, but there have been reports of throats being exercised in the same way in Cornwall and London. The word also appears in two novels set in Worcestershire by Frances Brett Young and in a short story of Devonshire by L. A. G. Strong. Other places tend to spell it "tizzack".

Old favourite "fair ter middlin", a stock response in Norfolk to general inquiries about state of health, was also a regular response from the Dorset farm worker of the 1920's.

"Highlows," leather ankle boots for wet weather, were also 18th century military boots and are mentioned as such in Thackeray's novel "The Virginians".

There are many other cases where "Norfolk words" have to be shared with other areas and other times. But we do give them our own special treatment.

So, no firm rules - and plenty of variations and exceptions just when you think you might have found some! Why on earth do enthusiasts continue to write in their local language when they start with so many handicaps?

Perhaps the answer is tied up in affection. Dialect literature is written from the heart and that can bring all barriers crashing down.

Lesson Two Exercises

✧ Pick a sentence at random from your newspaper or favourite book and turn it into 'Norfolk'. Do this daily until you feel at ease with the idea.

✧ As you travel around the county listen how certain words and phrases are given different sounds. Write examples down where possible.

Lesson Three - Ignore The Rumours!

The Norfolk dialect has been directed towards the obituary columns for the best part of two centuries - so any fresh claims about it being on the way out should be taken with a hundredweight of salt.

Even the most ardent champions have mixed extreme caution bordering on fatalism with their praise and illumination. The Rev. Robert Forby, whose extensive "Vocabulary of East Anglia" remains the richest source of local delights, thought he was launching a final flourish as he compiled it in the early years of the 19th century. The scholarly parson sized up popular dialects in his introduction and lamented: "Will they not be overwhelmed and borne down by the general onset of the various plans and unwearied extertions for the education of all?"

Harry Cozens-Hardy, who edited the first "Broad Norfolk" booklet published in 1893 from letters sent to the Eastern Daily Press, prophesied the dialect would die out within a generation under the influence of the Board schools.

Exactly a century later, a special Eastern Daily Press survey sent out an uplifting message - "There is a future for the Norfolk dialect!". An editorial headlined "Demise is Squit" began proudly: "Twain-like, reports of the demise of the Norfolk dialect have been greatly exaggerated."

It said the survey showed a remarkable resilience confirming that the dialect had a future which the National Curriculum Council should recognise. "The council for good and obvious reasons wants to encourage spoken standard English. But dialect is a legitimate and honourable element of good speech, a vigorous and enhancing dimension that should be prized and encouraged. The enemy of sound speech is not genuine dialect, but a rootless babble, or as we say with Norfolk succinctness, 'squit'."

The 1993 survey, the first serious attempt to gauge the strength of the dialect for many years, asked readers to identify 20 dialect words. It was completed by 239 adults and 242 children.

Language expert Professor Peter Trudgill, from Norwich, said: "Norfolk people will always be speaking in a way which distinguishes them from London and the Midlands. I do think there is a future for the Norfolk dialect. It resides as much in the grammar and pronunciation as anything else."

The survey was prompted by fears that the National Curriculum Council wanted

---

A MATTER OF ...

There had been a sudden death in the village, and two Norfolk mawthers were discussing it ...

"Ent that a'rummun ... there's ole Mrs Carter woss bin ailin' for years, an' she's still alive, an' poor ole Aggie Smith wunt hardly ill a week..."

"Well, thass how that go. Sum people die all of a suddin, an' sum onnem live till the werry larst momint!"

teachers to force all children to speak standard English - even in the playground. Critics feared the move could sound the death knell for local dialects in general.

Although the over-60s predictably came out on top with an average of 75 per cent, children fared better than expected. Thetford schoolgirl Amy Crystal scored 17 out of 20.

Historian Aime Carter remembered a time when many of the words in the survey were used regularly. She scored 18 out of 20 and was the only person who correctly identified both nanny dishwasher (also known as polly dishwasher) and swift. "I came to Norfolk as a probation officer 47 years ago and covered about seven courts. I first became interested in dialect because a lot of my clients were really broad Norfolk."

A big crop of letters followed the survey and its results, most of the correspondents to the EDP warming to the survival cause despite natural fears that it would continue to be diluted as the county becomes more cosmopolitan.

A passionate call for determined efforts to keep something of our heritage came from Jenny Barker of Ludham, whose grandfather was the celebrated traditional folk-singer Harry Cox. His voice was heard by English folk enthusiasts all over the world thanks to recordings. He died in 1971.

"I am sure that if he were alive now people would not understand him at all! He had alternative words for just about everything" said Jenny, adding that her children spoke fewer of the old words than she did.

For all the doubts and misgivings, dialect-lovers can derive some comfort from the fact we've heard it all before - many times. Norfolk affection and resilience should ensure the debate is taken with relish deep into the 21st century. All rumours to the contrary must be measured against all those plans for premature burials.

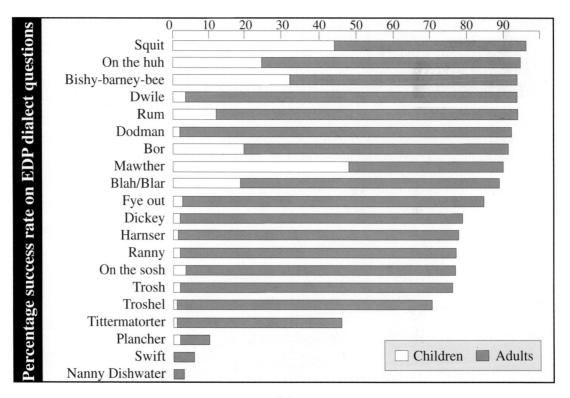

Percentage success rate on EDP dialect questions

	Children	Adults

Squit, On the huh, Bishy-barney-bee, Dwile, Rum, Dodman, Bor, Mawther, Blah/Blar, Fye out, Dickey, Harnser, Ranny, On the sosh, Trosh, Troshel, Tittermatorter, Plancher, Swift, Nanny Dishwater

How many did you know?

Average % marks across the age groups

Adults

Under 30:	**30%**
30-60:	**70%**
Over 60:	**75%**
Average:	**58%**

Children

Primary:	**9.5%**
Secondary:	**18%**
Average:	**13.5%**

Squit: talking nonsense; also a squirt or syringe
On the huh: awry, slanted or not level
Bishy-barney-bee: a ladybird
Dwile: a course rag used as a dishcloth or floorcloth
Rum: curious, strange, funny, odd, peculiar
Dodman: garden snail (also: Dodoman)
Bor: neighbour or boy
Mawther: young woman, tomboy
Blah/Blar: to weep or cry loudly
Fye out: clean out (often ditches or dykes)
Dickey: a donkey (also: Dicky)
Harnser: heron (there are about 40 other spellings)
Ranny: any small rodent, but usually a shrew
On the sosh: sloping or slanting
Trosh: to thresh (also: Throsh)
Troshel: threshold (also: Throsel and Trostle)
Tittermatorter: see-saw (American: Teeter totter)
Plancher: a boarded floor in upstairs room
Swift: a newt
Nanny Dishwasher: a pied wagtail

Lesson Three Exercises

✧   Use the EDP survey to test friends and relatives on their knowledge of dialect words - as soon as you have got them all correct..

✧   Seek out an elderly resident native in your locality and ask how the dialect has changed in his or her lifetime. It may be useful to use a tape recorder.

Lesson Four - Mind The Double Negative!

The danger of attaching "as a rule" to any part of the Norfolk vocabulary cannot be stressed too often. But those seeking guidance through an intricate maze are advised to accept the wisdom of this profound statement: Norfolk people swallow their consonants, do strange things with their vowels and are incapable of rolling an 'r' or dealing with a round 'o'.

A useful starting point. It was put in a far more erudite way by our old friend the Rev. Robert Forby in the introduction to his "Vocabulary of East Anglia" in 1830: "The most general and pervading characteristic of our pronunciation, which may, indeed, be called the essential character, is a narrowness and tenuity, precisely the reverse of the round, sonorous, 'mouth-filling' tones of Northern English. The broad and open sounds of vowels, the rich and full tones of diphthongs, are generally thus reduced."

We'll look at some of the sounds in more detail in the final lesson. Here it is useful to feature a few of the idiosyncrasies running through the vernacular, accepting with good grace that some may have been designed to confuse the furriner!

A Norfolk penchant for answering one question with another can both amuse and annoy. Only in extreme cases does it move to anger. "How are you feeling today?" will draw a cautious "I dunt rightly know, dew I?", or "I hev bin in bed orl week, hent I?"

Before Radio Norfolk opened in 1980 I recall a newcomer to the county returning to the studio anxious to share a real gem he had collected on his recording rounds. He asked a local lad to say what Norfolk might be like after a nuclear explosion. Allowing his imagination full rein, the boy replied: "Wuh, thass a' gorn ter be jist like wun gret big tip, ent it?" There's no answer to that, is there?

Another little linguistic trick the native can play is to end a response just as it's getting to the interesting bit.

For example, the inquiry "Are you coming this evening?" has been known to prompt a measured "Well, that orl depend". Depends upon what? Household chores? Transport arrangements? The cost of living? Chances are you'll never know.

Perhaps the most traditional inquiry "Are yew gorter cum?" might be blessed with a more enlightening reply.

Beware words and expressions that might mean the opposite to what they say. (You don't have to be a politician to try that one). "Doubt" can be used in the most peculiar manner; "I doubt he 'oont go" really means "I'm quite certain he won't go".

The word "funny" carries a different flavour in Norfolk, meaning "extremely", as in "Thass a funny good hoss!"

"Without" becomes "unless" in explanations like "He wunt go without I give him a quid ter spend". When a Norfolk man says "Fare y'well, tergether" with all the fondness he can muster he is referring to all present, whether singly or in a crowd.

Use of the double negative is very popular. An old chap on the farm complaining because he couldn't find anyone to lend a hand was heard to exclaim: "Thass the wast o' this here place - there ent never nobody ter help nobody wi' noffin'!"

Absence of the third person singular present tense is commonplace: "He go" and "He say" are prime examples. Use of the verb "do" as a conjunction comes out in references like "Yew'd better go ter bed dew yew'll be tired in the mornin'." Look out for the additional use of the preposition "on" as in "I'm a'dewin' on it".

Norfolk people make liberal use of the "historic present" as in "He see yew a'cummin'." A fascinating conjugation of verbs can be found in the old Norfolk description of a hard winter: "Fust that friz, then that snew, then the thew, an' then that tanned ryte rownd an' friz orl over agin."

An invitation to pay a call is "Cum yew up ter mine" or "Cum yew round ter ours". "Now" is another firm favourite. Rather than say "I'm just coming", a Norfolk man will pronounce "I'm now a'cummin'."

Remember, many words beginning with a "v" take a "w" start - warmint, willage and wittles among them - while the letter can also be changed in the middle of a word ... so "cultivating" becomes "cultiweartin'."

If the dialect itself is fundamentally Anglo-Saxon in origin, it has gathered many contributions from Danes and Vikings, Dutch, German and Norman invaders who came largely to pillage and plunder, as well as Dutch and Walloon weavers and Protestant and Huguenot refugees.

Norfolk can make similar capital out of more recent invasions to help keep the dialect going. After all, many of those earlier visitors who could have been confused by the way the natives spoke made the most of the old maxim - if you can't beat 'em, join 'em!

SHORE DOES!

An old Norfolk woman from the country went to the seaside for the first time. She looked at the waves and then asked a friend who was with her: "Do that allus keep a'muddlin' long like that?".

Lesson Four Exercises

✧   Write down some examples of the double negative you may encounter, and then transform them into orthodox English. Keep a tally on the number of times in a day you hear one question answered by another.

✧   Compile your own list of Norfolk words and expressions that don't mean what they say!

Lesson Five - Now Put It All Together!

While there remains a blatant shortage of phonetic symbols to do it proper justice, the Norfolk dialect demands efforts to reproduce vowel sounds heard nowhere else. Some will accuse the natives of unashamed laziness in not opening their mouths far enough when speaking, although one useful reply is that extreme care has to be taken against the prevailing east wind!

Individual habits and preferences spread colour as well as confusion, but the following pointers have done the rounds often enough to be taken as honest signposts through the linguistic jungle. How long it takes you to find a clearing could well depend on your powers of perseverance.

The sound of a Norfolk 'a', often rendered in writing as 'aa', rhymes with 'air' or 'care', but is well drawn out as in "Open yew that gearte, mearte, dew yew'll be tew learte."

A long 'e' can be changed into an 'a', so that 'beer' becomes 'bare' and 'three cheers' turns into 'three chairs'.

A short 'e' often becomes 'i', as in "Git yew out o' the way" or "I ent a' gorn hoome, not yit, I ent". Then it can be transformed into a short 'u', as when 'shed' becomes 'shud'.

A long 'i' tends to come out as 'oi':- "He wuz a' roidin' his boike".

You have been warned that a true Norfolk voice cannot manage a round 'o'. So invariably 'I hope' will come out as 'I hoop'. A 'road' is a 'rood', rhyming with 'wood' and 'roof' is in harmony with the 'woof' of a dog!

Shrewd judges say the Norfolk rendition of 'roof' is the biggest give-away among those who have the audacity to try to cover up their roots. Just to add more spice, a long 'o' can turn into a 'u', so 'moon' is 'mune' and 'fool' is 'fule'. Oh, don't forget the short

'o' can become a sort of long 'a', as in 'naathin' for 'nothing'; my preference is for 'noffin' in a vain bid to keep it relatively simple!

The sound of Norfolk's long 'u' has been compared with that of a French one. While refined ladies may be inclined to pronounce the word 'beautiful' as 'byootiful', a Norfolk woman says proudly, 'Thass bew'iful'.

'Don't' in Norfolk can become 'dorn't', although some prefer the sharper 'dunt'. 'Going' usually turns into 'gorn', as in "I ent a'gorn ter dew it". But 'I won't do it' changes to 'I oont dew it', with the 'w' being dropped. While the 'ts' are often left out altogether, occasionally 'th' becomes a hard 't' as in counting ... 'one, tew, t'ree'.

The 'h' at the beginning of a word is not usually dropped, but the 'g' at the end of a word is nearly always swallowed - 'sailing' and 'listening' becomes 'a'sailin'' and 'a'listenin''.

Don't forget how 'that', often turned into 'tha' or 'thass', is used extensively in place of 'the', 'this' and 'it'. 'They' regularly replaces 'those' or 'them', and 'theirselves' is used instead of 'themselves'.

Plurals are often shunned. An order for 'five ton o'coal' might be accompanied by the instruction, 'And take that ter where he live'.

The coalman might regret making a long trip merely to find no-one at home - "Blarst, I wunt a' went if I'd a'known!".

Don't confuse Broad Norfolk with Broad Norwich, which at worst has degenerated into what Jonathan Mardle called "an adenoidal gabble". One schoolmaster made a list of horrors he had encountered in the city classroom. That list included: 'Asswahreesay' (That's what he says); 'Owdsi'eegirron?' (How did the City get on?); and 'Woyyawahn?' (What do you want?).

Frightening examples of urban jargon not fit to stand alongside the durable and delightful Norfolk dialect!

Running words into one another produces many collisions that give little offence beyond the city boundaries. "Dunt peggarter orl his squit" is the colourful Norfolk manner of suggesting there is little point in paying regard to all his nonsense. "Betterannerhebbin" is a memorable response to any inquiry about state of health - or at least where "fair ter middlin'" will not suffice.

If you are no better than when you embarked on this perilous journey, take heart from the old Norfolk adage, "Dew yew keep a' troshin'!", go through all the lessons again - and find a friendly native to turn a light on the darkest corners.

Lesson Five Exercises

✦   Jot down examples you hear when words are run into each other, making a careful translation alongside.

✦   Write your own Norfolk item, prose or verse, and try it out on someone with real feeling for the dialect. Take all criticisms kindly - and move on to the next section to see how it is really done!

Section Two

Norfolk Stories and Verses

A LOT OF BULL

The village parson was surprised to meet in a narrow lane one of his smallest Sunday school pupils driving a large cow.
"Good morning, Mary. Where are your going with that enormous beast?"
"Please, sar, I'm a tearkin' ole Buttercup to be bulled."
"Dear me, but couldn't your father do that?"
"Oh no, sar ... that must be a bull."

There It Is!

Horry and Tom were strolling down the headland of a big field of barley stubble.

"Can yew see that ole hare over there?" asked Horry.

"No" said Tom, "my eyes arn't as good as yours."

"Well, jist yew look over that way as far as yew can see" said Horry. "Now can yew see it?"

"No" said Tom.

"Well, now look a little bit farther" said Horry, "and a little bit more tew the ryte - and there it is."

Colourful Words

"They're talkin' a' hainin' our wages agen", says Ben, referring to the discussion on a wage increase for farmworkers now under consideration. B.B.C. English may be the coming language. But how much poorer we shall be when it finally supersedes the colourful and expresive words provided by our dialects.

When Ben ploughs at right angles to his original work, he is working "overwart": if on the skew, he is "on the sosh". If a field is badly shaped, he refers to the odd awkward corners as "scutes", whilst a small field is a "pightle".

He walks home down the loke or drift (lane), below the hedge of which runs a "holl" (ditch), and every so often a grup leading into it (a narrow cut through the grass verge to run surface water from the road into the holl). As a rule he walks briskly enough, but sometimes he's simply pampling (strolling aimlessly). Occasionally he limps a little or "goes himpy". And though it takes a good deal to ruffle or upset him in the ordinary way, there are times when he gets into a real puckerterry.

To Ben withered or wilted vegetables are foosey or clung, a dishcloth is a dwile, a snail a dodman. A see-saw is a titter-ma-torter (his uncle made us one when we were children), sweets are cushies, a donkey a dickey, a young girl a mawther, a pigeon a dow, a fingerstall a hutkin.

He's always ready for a mardle (gossip), he tizzacks if he has a slight cough, and he bops (stoops) when he wants to pick up something he's dropped. Ben is never ill, he simply feels queer. His worn-out kettles and pails don't leak, they run. A storm is never a storm, but a tempest. And when he bids me good-bye, it is always "Fare-ye-well".

Elizabeth Harland, No Halt At Sunset, 1951

Norfolk Dumplin's Recipe

Yew put haalf a pound o' plaain flar in a
    bassin,
An' a haalf tea-spune o' baakin' powder
    tew;
Yew mix that up in haalf a pint o' water,
An' that maaake fower nice dumplin's,
    that that dew.

Yew pick 'em up and drop 'em in a sauce-
    pan,
Where yer vegetables 're b'ilin' wi' yer
    meat,
An' arter twenta minnits they'll be riddy,
An' yew're got a dinner what go down a
    treat!

John Kett.

A Good View

A Norfolk countryman was taken by a friend to see the sea. It was his first visit. His friend, looking north, informed him that it stretched away for hundreds of miles, probably as far as the North Pole.

"Oh, I daresay that dew!" exclaimed the labourer.

There was only the smoke of a steamer, low down on the horizon, to be seen.

The same night, back in his home pub, the labourer was telling another friend what he had seen. This time he was more outspoken: "I know thass a lie" he said, "cors I see'em a'troshin on th'uther bank!".

It's A Pushover

It was a warm moonlit night. After a busy week in the harvest field two local lads had sampled rather more than was good for them at the old Red Lion.

Standing near the open window of the tap room Bertie looked across the graveyard at the church, standing proud ancd clear by the light of the harvest moon.

At the chancel end only a few yards of grass and a narrow path separated the church from a steep bank falling down to the road.

"Less see if we kin push the chatch over that bank afore we go hoom" he said.

"Orl rite" replied Charlie, "I rekun we kin dew it, ole partner".

"Bet yew a pint yew carnt moove it" came the general chorus. The cheerful two made their way to the bottom of the tower and started pushing for all their worth.

"I'm gittin' tew hot" said Bertie, "Less tearke our jackits orff"

After another five minutes of hard pushing to no avail, Charlie suddenly put his finger in his mouth and held it up.

"Cor, blarst me! we're a'pushin' aginst the wind. We'd batter go rownd thuther ind an' push that way."

Off they went and renewed their efforts. In the meantime, old Tom nipped out of the Red Lion and took their jackets from the foot of the tower. He hid them under the seat in the bar.

After a while Bertie said: "I bleeve I hev dunnit, bor."

"That we hev" said Charlie. "Less go

back in now and git a pint."

They went round the tower end to collect their jackets.

"Well, I'll be b e g g a r e d ! " said Charlie "dammed if we hent pushed it right over our jackets. Now we'll hatter go an' push it back agin!"

Hay Hay!

They tell me thet hay is werra scarce,
Mearkin' a pound fer a little bale.
'Cors we know last spring wus hully wet,
Yit all the searme thass a sorra tale.

Thet jist go tu show wot I've allus said,
An' tu me thass true beyond doubt,
If yow mearke spare when yow've got plenta,
Yow'll allus hev some when yow run out.

Cyril Jolly.

Preaching The Word

Norfolk's village chapels have provided countless stories passed on with a great affection. Some of the old rural preachers may have been short on formal education, but they took some beating when it came to colourful and inventive language.

One local preacher had read the word "phenomenal" in his paper, but had never heard it actually spoken. So, in the course of his sermon he referred to the "fee-no-mean-al" love of God. One member of his congregation interrupted: "What do you mean by 'fee-no-mean-al'?".

"Well" said the preacher, "as I wuz a'cummin here this arternewn on my byke, I see a cow in a midder a'munchin' grass, and I hear a lark a'singin' up above. Now, if that lark had bin in the midder a'munchin' grass, and that there cow had bin a'singin' up above, that wood a'bin fee-no-mean-al!".

HAVE A BREAK

An old Norfolk woman decided to visit her son in Australia. A friend sympathised with her over the length of the journey. The old girl replied: "That 'ont be ser bad ... I'm gorn' ter break the janney at Diss."

Lazy Wind

I'm the on'y one on Cromer pier this
    February day,
An' what they call a lazy wind is whippin'
    up the spray;
That lazy wind, that crazy wind,
From icy seas come tew yer,
Tha's jus' tew lazy t'go round, an' so that
    go clean trew yer!

There's waves a-roarin' up the beach, wi'
    foam a-flyin' high,
An' wicket sheets o' bitin' sleet come
    swirlin' orf the sky.
Ah, yew may try t'hide away,
That wind'll still git near yer,
An' when that dew, that go right trew - ah,
    tha's enough t'fleer yer!

The sea come crashin' on the stones,
    there's snow there on the sand;
The wind get wuss; tha's now a gaale, an' I
    can hardly stand -
That bitin' wind, that fightin' wind,
Tha's healthy, so they say, bor;
There in't no germs on Cromer pier, tha's
    blew 'em all away, bor!

John Kett

Section Three

A Norfolk Dictionary

LOCAL LOGIC

The farmer turned to the lad who was late for work again.
"Dew yew know what tyme yew start work?"
"Yis ... bowt fyve minnits arter I git here."
"No, yew sorft young fewl ... why are yew learte?"
"Thass lyke this here, marster. When that wuz tyme ter cum ter wak,
I wuz asleep. I knew that wunt no good a'cummin then ... so I
wearted til I wook up!".

A Norfolk Dictionary

Abroad—*old Norfolk for outside: "Rough weather abroad, ole partner".*

Abser—*an abscess.*

Accordinlie—*accordingly - with emphasis on last syllable - "accordinlie to him".*

Ackulster—*axle.*

Addle—*to thrive, usually applied to crops.*

Afore—*before - "He dun that afore I got there".*

Afront—*in front - "Go yew on afront".*

Agin—*against - "I lent my bike agin the wall"; also again - "I sharnt dew that agin".*

Ahind—*behind - "I lent mine ahind it".*

Ahuh—*awry, lopsided. also "on the huh", "on the sosh" (qv), "on the slantendicular" (qv).*

Alonger me—*with me, as in "Are yew a'gorn ter hev a pynt alonger me?"*

Allus/allust—*always (pronounced ollus).*

Anend—*on end - "Raise that ladder anend".*

Annic—*to fool about, skywanicking (qv), nonnicking (qv).*

Angry—*painfully inflamed - "My corns ent harf angry".*

Arsle—*to move or wriggle backwards.*

Arter—*after - "I reckon she's arter suffin' ".*

Athwast/athort/acrosst—*across.*

A'top of—*upon - "I saw Mr Jones a'top of his new hoss".*

Atwin—*between.*

Avels—*awns of barley.*

Ax—*to ask. Past tense "axed" - original Saxon.*

Aylsham treat—*to treat yourself, pay your own way.*

Babbing—*fishing for eels, using as bait worms attached to worsted.*

Backstrike—*to plough backstrike is to plough land already turned so that it is turned back again.*

Backus—*outhouse or scullery (back-house). Here the "backus boy", the lowliest of servants, did most of his work.*

Badget—*badger.*

Badly—*in ill health.*

Bait—*food packed up and taken to work in the fields, mid- morning snack, elevenses, "dockey" (qv).*

Baldie-coot—*a coot, from the white patch on the bird's head, just above the beak.*

Balk—*ridge of land left unploughed.*

Bandy—*one of several county names for the hare - from the curvature of the hind legs.*

Beck

50

Bandy-wicket—*old name for cricket.*
Barley-bird—*the nightingale.*
Barleysel(e)—*season of growing barley.*
Barney—*argument, quarrel.*
Barrow-pig—*smallest of the litter also petman (qv) or pitman (qv).*
Bavins—*light, loose faggots.*
Bay-duck—*shell-duck, from its bright colour like a bay horse.*
Beat—*to mend fishing nets, hence "beatster" a net-mender.*
Beaver—*farm worker's afternoon snack.*
Beck—*a stream.*
Becomes—*best clothes, Sunday outfit.*
Bee-bird—*the great tit, so called because of its reputed partiality to bees.*
Beetle—*heavy wooden mallet.*
Beezlins—*cow's first milk after calving, a valuable ingredient in some old rural recipes.*
Beggary—*large growth of weeds in a field of corn or root vegetables.*

Begone—*decayed, worn out.*
Bein'as—*because of, on account of - "Bein'as thass a'rearnin, he ent a'cummin".*
Bents—*coarse, rough grass.*
Best part of sum tyme—*taking a fair while.*
Bestow—*store away or lay up for future use.*
Betterannerhebbin—*opposite to "wassanwotterwuz"*
Betty/betsy—*a kettle.*
Bezzle—*to drink greedily.*
Bibble—*of ducks, to search for food underwater.*
Biddles—*young chickens.*
Biffins—*variety of cooking apple.*
Biggoty—*overbearing, bossy.*
Billywix—*an owl, usually applied to the tawny species.*
Bishy-barney-bee—*a ladybird. Norfolk historian Walter Rye suggested it came from "Bene Bee" - blessed bee. Ted Ellis, doyen of local naturalists,*

Bishy-barney-bee

pointed out that ladybirds usually appear about St. Barnabas Day, June 23rd (old calendar).

Blee—*to reassemble, bear a likeness to - "That mawther (qv) dew blee her Aunty Polly, that she dew".*

Black stalk—*a chimney.*

Blar—*to cry, especially children.*

Blood-ulf—*a bullfinch.*

Bolders—*bullrushes.*

Boke—*bulk - "There's more boke than corn in that crop".*

Bolt—*1. to swallow food without chewing - "Dunt yew bolt yar grub ser quick"; 2. a bundle, particularly reeds used for thatching.*

Boodle/buddle—*the corn marigold.*

Bop—*to curtsey, squat, duck one's head to avoid being seen.*

Bor—*local form of address for males and, occasionally, females too, although they are usually "maw" or "mawther"* *(qv). Some suggest it is an abbreviation of "neighbour", but more likely it comes from Anglo-Saxon "bur" or "gebur", a householder or freeman, similar to the Dutch "Boer".*

Bosky—*tipsy, merry.*

Bottle-bump—*the bittern (or buttle).*

Bottle-nose—*the porpoise.*

Bottle-tom—*the long-tailed tit.*

Botty—*fussy, self-important - "She's a botty little mawther".*

Bough-load—*last load of harvested corn. It was customary to decorate it with leafy branches as it left the field.*

Braiding—*net-making.*

Brangle—*to argue or dispute.*

Brashy—*land overgrown with rushes.*

Brattlings—*loppings from felled trees.*

Brawn/braun—*a boar.*

Braze—*to braze out is to insist one is right in an argument.*

Bred and born—*Norfolk purists insist this is the proper order not "born and bred".*

Brief—*written or printed petition or begging paper.*

Brork/brortch—*to belch, to break wind.*

Brotch/broach—*short stick, pointed at one end, a hazel rod used for thatching.*

Bronickle—*bronchial. One of several mispronunciations.*

Bruff—*in good spirits, hearty.*

Brumbles—*brambles, general term for untidy undergrowth.*

Buckhead—*to cut off the top of overgrown hedge.*

Bud—*a calf beginning to show horns.*

Buffle—*muddle, confusion (buffle headed).*

Bulk—*to throb - "My sore thumb dunt harf bulk".*

Bull's noon—*midnight.*

Bumbaste—*to beat severely.*

Bumble-footed—*clumsy.*

Bunny—*bruise or swelling.*

Bunt—*to butt.*
Burr—*haze around the moon.*
Buskins—*leather leggings, gaiters.*
Butt—*a flounder.*

Caddow/cadder—*a jackdaw.*
Caffling—*hesitating.*
Caghanded—*left-handed or clumsy.*
Cail—*to throw weakly, wide of the mark.*
Call—*need or requirement -"Yew hent no call*
to git upset".
Canker—*caterpillar.*
Carney—*to wheedle, flatter, fawn upon.*
Carnser—*causeway or raised road.*
Carr—*a clump of trees.*
Cat's ice—*thin ice with air trapped beneath it.*
Caution—*remarkable event or surprising*
news - "Well, if that ent a caution!".
Cavings—*refuse from threshing.*
Cedar—*a pencil.*
Chalder/scalder—*a large number.*
Chates—*scraps of food.*

Cheat—*detachable shirt front, dicky.*
Chelp—*cheek, insolence.*
Chick—*to germinate.*
Chife—*a small piece.*
Chimble—*to slice or cut into small pieces.*
Chimbley—*chimney - also "chimley"*
Chip up—*to improve in health or circumstances.*
Chitter—*noise made by a cornered rat.*
Chitterlings—*pig's entrails cleaned and fried.*
Chovy—*cockchafer or beetle.*
Chummy—*soft felt hat with a narrow brim.*
Churky—*under-cooked vegetables which are crunchy are said to be churky.*
Clag—*to clean or comb out matted hair.*
Claggy—*sticky or lumpy.*
Clammed—*very hungry.*
Clamp—*heap of potatoes or beet, covered with straw and earth to keep out frost.*
Clarty—*daubed with syrup or juice.*
Clawth/clorth—*severe pain - "That tooth dew gi'me sum clawth!".*

Clever—*special meaning in Norfolk of handsome or dexterous.*
Clinker—*above average - "Weer got sum rare clinkers ter year".*
Clip—*slight blow or cuff - "Clip o'the lug".*
Clote—*the coltsfoot.*
Clunch—*lump of chalk used in building.*
Clung—*dried up or shrivelled, usually fruit or vegetables.*
Coach—*to stroke or fondle a cat or other pet.*
Coarse—*as opposed to fine as in "a coarse morning".*
Cob—*a seagull - and a horse (inland).*
Cocky—*a drain or small stream.*
Coddy—*stuck up, proud.*
Colder—*brick rubble.*
Come-back—*the guinea-fowl, from its call.*
Cooms—*ridges formed between horse tracks and wheel ruts.*
Cooshies/cushies—*sweets.*
Cop—*to throw a short distance.*

Cop-a-hold—*to catch* - *"Cop-a-hold o' that ball!"*

Coped—*muzzled (referring to ferrets).*

Copper-jack—*odd-job boy, main duty to look after the old copper boiler.*

Coquilles—*spiced buns eaten on Shrove Tuesday and Easter, particularly in the Norwich area.*

Cor, blarst me!—*favourite Norfolk expletive along "Well. I'll be blowed!" lines.*

Corf—*cough.*

Coughwort—*the coltsfoot.*

Crimbling—*to creep about sneakily.*

Crome—*muck-rake or implement with curved tines for clearing ditches or lifting root crops.*

Crowd—*to push along or drive forward - "He dint harf crowd his ole byke up the hill!".*

Crow-keeping—*bird scaring.*

Cruckle—*a crust (to grate or creak in Suffolk).*

Crud-barrer—*wheelbarrow.*

Cubelow—*cupola, chimney of a malting.*

Cuckoo—*cocoa* - *"I hev a cup o'cuckoo afore I go ter bed".*

Cup—*command to a horse to go left when ploughing etc. (probably an abbreviation of "come up").*

Custard—*smack or blow.*

Cut—*1. a blow* - *"I'll gi'yew a cut o'the skull!" 2. a picture.*

Cuter/kewter—*money.*

Dabster—*expert in some particular field.*

Dag—*dew or mist.*

Daggly—*damp, ragged.*

Damnified—*indemnified* - *"That ent no matter ter him, he's damnified".*

Daneswort—*elderweed.*

Dannies—*a child's hands.*

Dannocks—*1. hedging gloves; 2. small cakes of dough.*

Dans—*year old lambs.*

Dardledumdew—*helpless or feckless person.*

Dark over Will's mother's—*bad weather coming. Will's mother not confined to Norfolk.*

Datty—*dirty.*

Dauby—*sticky, muddy after rain.*

Dawg/dorg—*dog.*

Deen—*a faint sound, usually used in the negative sense - "He never med a deen when he cum in".*

Deke/dike—*ditch, or in some areas, a bank.*

Develin—*a swift, possibly from devil-bird because of its very dark plumage and swift flight.*

Dew—*1. social occasion or function - "We hed a rare good dew down the pub"; 2. to thrive or succeed - "His arly tearters dunt fare ter dew t'year"; 3. does, as in "dew the sun shine?".*

Dibles—*difficulties, complications.*

Dickadilver—*the periwinkle flower.*

Dickadilver

57

Dickey—*a donkey.*

Diddleton Frank—*a heron, from Didlington in West Norfolk and the call of the heron (see also Harnser).*

Didle—*1. a ditching spade; 2. to dig or clean out.*

Didopper—*the little grebe, probably from its quaint diving habits.*

Dindle/dingle—*sowthistle.*

Ding—*slap or blow - "Ding o'the lug".*

Dingin'—*showery.*

Dingle—*opposite of make haste.*

Dint—*did not - "I dint dew it".*

Dipper—*handled receptacle for dipping water from a butt etc.*

Disimprove—*to weaken or deteriorate.*

Dissables—*underwear, from the French deshabille.*

Dockey—*labourer's dinner, taken to the field in a dockey bag.*

Doddle—*a pollard tree.*

Dodman

Dodman—*a snail (also hodmadod, with variations in many parts of Britain).*
Doke—*dent or hole.*
Dop—*short, quick curtsey.*
Dop-a-low(ly)—*used to describe a short, squat person.*
Doss—*1. to toss; 2. hassock.*
Dow—*wood pigeon.*
Drant—*to drawl one's words.*
Draw—*to clean out a dyke.*
Draw along—*move slowly.*
Draw-latch—*crafty or sneaky person.*
Draw-water—*the goldfinch.*
Drift—*a lane.*
Drug—*vehicle for carrying felled trees.*
Dudder—*to shiver - "all of a dudder".*
Dullar—*loud noise - "The boys dunt harf kick up a dullar"*
Dumduckerdumer—*mixture of various colours, so faded as to be indescribable.*

Dumpling-hunter—*old-fashioned label for a hungry local preacher.*
Dunnock—*hedge sparrow.*
Durst/dast—*to dare (negative "I dassent").*
Dutfin—*bridle or halter for a horse.*
Duzzy—*stupid - "Yew duzzy yung fewl!".*
Dwany/dwainy—*weak and sickly.*
Dwile—*a floorcloth.*
Dwinged—*shrivelled (usually applied to fruit).*

Early-peep—*twitch grass.*
Ecclester—*axle tree of wagon or cart.*
Eldern—*elder tree.*
Elijahs/'lijahs—*string tied round labourer's trousers just below the knee. Also known as Yorks or Yorkers.*
Enow—*enough.*
Erriwiggle—*earwig.*
Esh—*ashtree.*
Ewe—*past tense of "owe" - "I ewe him ten quid".*

Erriwiggle

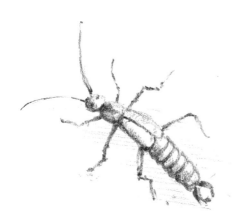

Faines—*ghostly creatures once reported in the Hethersett area.*

Fair ter midlin'—*stock response to inquiries about state of health.*

Fall—*a veil.*

Fang—*to seize hold of - "She fanged hold o'me!"*

Fapes/thapes—*gooseberries.*

Fare—*to feel or seem - "He allus fare ter cum learte" - "I dunt fare tew sharp terday".*

Fare y'well, tergether—*a fond goodbye. "Tergether" refers to all present, whether singly or in a crowd.*

Farlans—*shallow troughs used in the gutting of herring.*

Farrissee—*fairy (also pharissee).*

Fathom—*1. bundle of reeds for thatching; 2. to fill out or expand, referring to crops.*

Faut—*fault.*

Felfit—*fieldfare.*

Fie/fey/feign—*to fie out means to clean or scrape.*

Fierce—*1. fit, healthy; 2. inflamed, of a wound or skin infection.*

Filler/thiller—*shaft horse in a team.*

Fillister—*carpenter's tool for cutting grooves or rebuting.*

Finnicking—*too particular, fussy.*

Fintums—*fuss over food.*

Firplen—*dustpan.*

Fisherate—*to provide for, or perform a duty (probably from officiate).*

Fitten—*feet.*

Flag—*a tuft of grass.*

Flag-fire—*bonfire.*

Flair—*to skin a rabbit.*

Flapper—*a young wild duck.*

Flash—*to cut a hedge.*

Flasher—*a hedge-cutting tool.*

Fleer—*local pronunciation of "flay" - to remove a skin or hide. Often heard in connection with cold weather - "That ole east wind, thass enuff ter fleer yer!".*

Fleet—*shallow, or a dyke or shallow pool.*

Fleeten—*to make shallow.*

Fligger—*fidget.*

Floater—*1. heavy fall of rain; 2. type of dumpling.*

Fog/fob—*marsh grass.*

Foison—*juiciness of herbage - "There's plenty of foison in the hay".*

Foisty—*stale, mildewed (also fusty, feisty, fosey, ficety).*

Fold-pritch—*tool for making holes when putting up sheep enclosures.*

Foosey—*a withered vegetable, usually a turnip or radish.*

Foreigner/furriner—*anyone not a native of the vicinity!*

Forgive—*to thaw.*

Fowlete—*crossroads.*

Fourses/farses—*afternoon snack in the harvest field.*

Frail—*shallow basket made of rushes.*
Frame—*to put on airs.*
Frank—*heron, (see Didlington Frank and Harnser).*
Frawn—*frozen.*
Frazzle—*to unravel wool etc.*
Frazzled—*frayed or worn.*
Frenchman—*French or red-legged partridge.*
French mavis—*redwing.*
Fresher—*small frog.*
Frit—*frightened.*
Friz—*frozen.*
Froise—*to fry. Also a pancake.*
Frumple—*rumple.*
Fulfer—*missel-thrush.*
Full-flopper—*young bird ready to fly.*
Funny—*remarkable - "That rained funny hard last night".*
Fumble-fisted—*clumsy.*
Furrow-chuck—*whinchat.*

Fresher

Gaddy-wenting—*gossiping.*

Gain—*handy, advantageous.*

Galleting—*driving flint flakes between flints when building, to prevent weathering and to improve the appearance.*

Gallus-droply—*dirty or unhappy appearance.*

Galver—*to throb.*

Gammarattle—*nonsense, rubbish.*

Gan—*gave, given.*

Gansey/garnsey—*jersey.*

Gant—*a fair in the village.*

Gape-seed—*"He like his gape-seed" means he often stands and stares.*

Garp/gorp—*to gape or stare.*

Gastless—*stupid, thoughtless.*

Gast—*barren,- "A gast mare".*

Gather—*become inflamed.*

Gavel—*sheaf of carn before it is tied up, and a bundle of straw for the thatcher.*

Gays—*illustrations,- "He like ter look at the gays in the pearper".*

Get—*of a watch or clock, to gain.*

Gimbling—*sniggering.*

Git late earlier—*nights are pulling in.*

Gladden—*wild iris or yellow flag.*

Gloat/glat—*eel.*

Goat-sucker—*nightjar, from belief that these birds sucked milk from goats.*

Golden drop—*yellow plum.*

Goldering—*giggling, - "Stop yar goldering, bor!".*

Golpin/Gollerpin—*swallow quickly, gulping it down,- "He's golpin his grub".*

Good tidy—*satisfactory, reasonable. (Or tidy good).*

Gorn—*going,- "I ent a'gorn ter dew it!".*

Goslings—*willow catkins.*

Gotch—*jug or ewer.*

Go-ter-meetin'-clothes—*best or Sunday garb.*

Grane—*to strangle or suffocate.*

Greenulf—*greenfinch.*

Gret—*great,- "Thas a gret ole mountain".*

Goslings

Greybird—*English partridge.*
Grip/gripple—*small drain or water course.*
Groundsels—*foundations of a building.*
Grundle—*narrow, sunken trackway.*
Grunny—*a pig's snout.*
Grup—*shallow drain or rut.*
Guler—*yellowhammer.*
Gushy—*gusty, very windy.*
Guzunder—*chamberpot (guzunder the bed!)*

Ha and hacker—*to stutter.*
Hack-slavering—*talking in an excited way.*
Haddle—*hurdle.*
Hain—*to raise, especially in respect of wages or prices.*
Hakes—*hooks on which pots were hung by the fire, hence the expression "black as the hakes".*
Haller/holler—*to shout.*
Half-six/sixer—*derogatory term applied to a pretentious person, may come from "half past six", suggesting such an*

individual lay in bed for half an hour after the working man began his labours.

Hamper—*to damage.*

Hank (up)—*to fasten a gate or door.*

Hap—*to wrap.*

Hapt(on)—*met up with, come upon by chance. Also "happened acrorst"*

Harnser—*the heron.*

Harriage—*confusion. Probably from "harry", to harass or lay waste. "Gone to harriage" - gone to rack and ruin. Sometimes, erroneously, Harwich or Harridge.*

Harry the Denchman—*the carrion crow, from Harry the Danishman, better known as Harold Harefoot, son of King Canute.*

Harvest festivals—*large bloomers to inspire a chorus of "All is safely gathered in".*

Haunt—*a ghost.*

Hayjack—*whitethroat.*

Haysel—*haymaking season.*

Haze—*to put out in the sun to dry.*

Heater-piece—*triangular piece of ground, such as a grass area at a road junction.*

Hedge Betty—*hedge sparrow. Also hedgeman.*

Hen's noseful—*a very small amount.*

Here and there—*handy, or tidy and ship-shape.*

Herne—*part of one parish projecting into another.*

Herring-spink—*goldcrest.*

Het—*heated.- "Hev Mary het that kettle yit?".*

Hid—*head.- "Mind yer hid,boy".*

Hidlands—*headlands - the outside of a field.*

Higgle—*to argue or bargain.*

Higgler—*a dealer.*

High-larned—*well-educated.*

Highlow—*leather ankle boots for wet weather.*

Highsprite—*ghost.*

Highstrikers—*hysterics.*

Hilda—*elder.*

Himp—*to limp. Himpy-lame.*

Hin—*hen.*

Hinderpart—*the back of anything.*

Hips—*corners of a stack.*

Hissen/hisself—*himself.*

Hitch(up)—*to make room on a seat etc.*

Hive—*basket trap for eels.*

Hobby—*a pony.*

Hock—*to kick or trip up.*

Hodmedod—*snail (see dodman - more popular in Norfolk).*

Hog line—*"Brought up on a hog line" means badly brought-up, uncouth and ill mannered.*

Hold—*to be in possession of money - "Dew yew hold, bor, we'll go ter the pub".*

Hold-ye—*call of the boy (hold-ye boy) in charge of the horses drawing loads of corn sheaves in the harvest field - a warning to the man on top of the load. Also "howdgee", "howd" for the man in the load, "gee" for horse to go on.*

Hold yew hard!—*Hang on a moment.*

Holl—*ditch or dykes or a hole.*

Hollow-meat—*poultry, rabbit - other than butcher's meat.*

Holy Boys—*Royal Norfolk Regiment, probably originating from the Peninsular War, when the enemy thought that figures of Britannia (the regimental badge) were the Virgin Mary.*

Honky—*temper.*

Horfling—*moving clumsily.*

Horkey—*social gathering and feast to celebrate end of harvest.*

Horkey-load—*last load of harvest.*

Hornpie—*lapwing.*

Hoss—*1. horse; 2. to act boisterously, "hossin' about"; 3. to hurry, "Blarst, he cum hossin' along!".*

Holl

Housen—*houses.*

Hovers—*floating masses of water-weeds.*

Howin'an'mowin—*chattering, gossiping.*

Howsomever—*however.*

Huckabuck—*leapfrog.*

Hucker—*to complain or to stutter (see "ha and hacka").*

Hudderin—*large and unwieldy, usually applied to awkward youth.*

Huddle—*to pass the leg of a rabbit through the sinews of the other to enable it to be carried easily.*

Huh—*crooked or slanting - "On the huh".*

Hulk—*to skin and gut a rabbit.*

Hull—*to throw - "Hull that ball over here".*

Hull up—*to be sick, vomit.*

Hulver—*holly.*

Hummer—*a lie.*

Hunnycart—*posh folk call it the night-soil collection vehicle. Other down-to-earth labels include "lavender cart" and "violet wagon".*

Ivory

Hurch—*to push or shove.*
Hungry Ninth—*another nickname for the Royal Norfolk Regiment, said to result from an occasion when the soldiers of the 9th Regt. of Foot sold their Bibles to buy food.*
Hutkin/hudkin—*a case or sheath for a sore finger.*
Huxter/huxterer—*dealer.*

Ickeny—*an adjective, emphasis on the first syllable, used in Norfolk to describe anyone who is aggravating or difficult to deal with. Could it come from "Iceni" who aggravated the Romans in East Anglia?!*
Imitate—*to attempt, make an effort.- "I shunt imitate ter dew that if I wuz yew".*
Iron-hards—*purple loosestrife. Name comes from the tough roots of this attractive fenland flower, which were sometimes*

described as "shovel benders" by men clearing dykes.

Ivory—*ivy.*

Jacob—*a frog.*

Jag—*term applied to a quantity of flints or other stones equal to about 15 cwt.*

Jam—*to plod or walk heavily, or stamp on.*

Jannock—*fair, honest.*

Jargon—*what healthy Norfolk people do before breakfast - go a'jargon!*

Jatter—*to shake or knock.*

Jibbuck—*to shake up and down.*

Jiffling—*fidgeting.*

Jill-hooter—*owl.*

Jimmers—*hinges made of leather, often used on sheds or rabbit hutches.*

Jinks—*five-stones or "jacks" played by children.*

Jip—*aggravation, annoyance in the sense of pain - "That give me sum jip".*

Jill-hooter

Job—*anything remarkable - "Her new hat wunt harf a job!"*.

Jollificeartions—*fun, joviality.*

Jonamy Jones—*a pig, neither obviously male nor female.*

July razor—*a scythe.*

Jumpin'jacks—*frogs.*

Jurisdiction—*management, - "My man hev jurisdiction o'that".*

Kail—*to throw.*

Kedgy—*agile, sprightly, used with reference to the elderly.*

Keeler/killer—*wooden tub used for scalding a pig after killing. Also applied to large tubs used for washing and brewing.*

Keppier-holt—*instructions to a horse to go left.*

Keptathometogoataterin'—*excuse in note sent to teacher by a Norfolk mother. She had kept her son at home so he could help pick potatoes.*

Kelter—*condition or state, - "His farm's in good kelter".*

Kiderer—*pork butcher.*

Kinder—*kind of.*

Kinder-kinder—*not in the best of health.*

King George—*peacock butterfly. Also applied to red admiral and tortoiseshell.*

King Harry—*gold finch.*

Kiss-me-at-the-garden-gate—*pansy.*

Kit—*a fish basket.*

Kittywitches—*cockchafer beetles. Also "women of lowest order" who once begged in streets of Yarmouth wearing disguises.*

Knap—*to shape flints, - flint knapping.*

Knap-kneed—*knock-kneed.*

Knockin' an' toppin'—*how the farmworkers harvested sugarbeet before mechanisation. They knocked*

the beet together to remove the soil
then sliced off the leaves with a hook.

Know—*information, knowledge, - "Where
dew he git all his know?".*

Koished—*thrashed.*

Kyish—*looking smug or shy.*

Laid—*of corn, flattened by storms. Also
ponds or broads frozen hard.*

Lam—*to beat, - "He dint harf lam inter
him!".*

Lamper along—*take big strides. Also lope.*

Lanner—*whiplash.*

Larding—*a beating.*

Largesse—*gift of money at harvest-time.*

Larn—*(i.e. learn) to teach - "That'll larn
yer!".*

Lash/lashy—*watery or soft, often applied to
egg with soft shell.*

Last o' the meddlers—*a remark usually
made to over-inquisitive children,*

Livelong

Loke

meaning something like "curiosity killed the cat".

Latch—*to catch on or become entangled.*

Latch-lifter—*small sum of money, just enough to buy a drink, i.e. enter the door of the pub.*

Leasty—*damp, drizzly.*

Lickup—*small quantity, dollop, as if it were no more than the cat can lick up by one stroke of the tongue.*

Lig—*to pull or drag along.*

Ligger—*1. a plank bridge over a ditch; 2. short rod used in ridge thatching; 3. item of fishing tackle, usually used when pike or eel fishing.*

Lijahs—*straps round the trousers, just below the knees.*

Lints—*fishing nets.*

Livelong—*dandelion.*

Lode—*man-made water course.*

Loke—*lane or alley, usually enclosed.*

Lollop—*to progress slowly.*

Lond—*small piece of land, part of a divided plot.*
Long-dog—*a greyhound.*
Lucom—*a dormer window or barn slit.*
Lumberin'—*a noise.*
Lummox—*clumsy or ungainly person.- "Git yew out o' the way, yew gret lummox!".*

Malted—*hot and sweaty.*
Mank—*to toy with food. See also "pingle".*
March-birds—*frogs (corruption of marsh-birds).*
Mardle—*1. to gossip, chat at leisure; 2. a village pond.*
Mardlins—*duckweed or ducklings.*
Marrams—*coastal sand dunes planted with marram grass to prevent erosion.*
Mash/mesh—*marsh.*
Master—*expreses admiration. - "Thass a master gret howse".*

Mawkin

Masterpiece—*astonishing. - "Well, I shunt never ha'believed it. Thass a masterpiece!".*

Matchly—*corresponding, well-fitting.*

Matters—*to feel "no matters" means out-of-sorts, poorly.*

Mavis/mavish—*song-thrush.*

Maw/mor—*local form of greeting for women-folk.*

Mawkin—*a scarecrow.*

Mawther—*girl or young woman. - "She's a nice young mawther".*

Mazy—*1. sickly; 2. description of shotten or inferior herring.*

Meals—*sand-dunes.*

Meager/mearger—*long handled reap hook for cutting weeds.*

Meece/meezen—*mice.*

Merrimills—*sand hills.*

Merrymay—*mayfly or dragonfly.*

Midder—*meadow.*

Middlin'—*in fairly good health. - "fair ter middlin'".*

Midnight woman—*midwife.*

Milestone inspector—*gentleman of the road, a tramp*

Miller—*moth.*

Million—*pumpkin.*

Mine—*"She come to mine" instead of "She came to my house". Similarly with his, yours etc. "He come up ours Saturday an' we go round his o'Sundays".*

Mingins—*gnats, midges.*

Minifer—*stoat or weasel (cf ermine).*

Minify—*to make little of - opposite to magnify!*

Misery—*severe pain. - "She suffer with a misery in har stummick".*

Mislen-bird—*fieldfare.*

Mislen-bush—*mistletoe.*

Mite—*a little bit. - "I dew fare a mite hungry".*

Mitchamador—*cockchafer beetle.*

Mizzle—*drizzle.*

Mob—*to scold, tell off.- "She dint harf mob them kids".*

Mocking—*placed or planted alternatively, in rows, especially trees in orchards.*

Moderate—*in health, not too well.*

Moise—*to thrive, get better.*

Moll—*a mole.*

Monge—*to eat greedily.*

Morfrey/morphrey—*tumbril which could be converted into a wagon. (cf hermaphrodite).*

Mort—*a large number (probably from Icelandic fishermen).*

Morth— *a moth.*

Mouse-hunt—*a stoat.*

Mow in—*join in.*

Mucher—*something of good quality. Usually used in the negative - "That there ent a mucher".*

Muckup—*a manure heap.*

Muckwash—*hot and bothered - "all of a muckwash".*

Muddled—*referring to the moon, partly hidden by cloud.*

Mud-scuppit—*long handled scoop for cleaning out ditches.*

Muir-hearted—*tender hearted or easily moved.*

Mumpers—*carol singers or performers of traditional plays at Christmas. In Norwich beggars went mumping on St. Stephen's Day.*

Nailer—*determined or domineering person.*

Nanny Dishwasher—*pied wagtail (also Polly Dishwasher).*

Nasty-particular—*fastidious, precise.*

Native—*place of birth - "He hent never left his native".*

Neat'us/nettus—*cattle shed.*

Neck'un—*neckerchief.*

Neesen—*nest of birds.*

Neat'us

Nest-gulp—*smallest bird in the nest.*
Nevvy—*nephew.*
Nice—*fussy, particular*
Nijerting—*acting as midwife.*
Noah's arms—*cumulus clouds.*
Nobby—*a young colt.*
Noggin—*brickwork between timbers in buildings.*
Nointer—*rascal.*
Nonnicking—*fooling about, horseplay.*
Norweigan bishops—*towering thunder clouds (beeskeps)*
Nosings—*white quadrants painted on bows of wherries.*
Numb-chance—*stupid. - "Lookin' like numb-chance in a saw-pit" means looking lost or vacant when action is called for.*
Nye—*brood of pheasants.*

Oat flights—*chaff from oats.*
Old Year's Nyte —*New Year's Eve.*

Olive—*oyster-catcher.*
Ollands—*old pastures ploughed up for crop growing.*
One journey—*working without stopping for meals.*
Oven-bird—*bluetit or long-tailed tit, from shape of the nest.*
Overgive—*to thaw.*
Overwart—*athwart or across, with reference to harrowing land.*
Owler—*old term for a smuggler of wool.*

Packrag Day—*old Michaelmas day - moving day for many on account of change of employment.*
Paddock/puddock—*toad.*
Page—*boy assisting a shepherd*
Paigle/pagle—*cowslip.*
Painted ladies—*applied to kippers after they had been dyed before being smoked.*
Pamment—*paving stone or pavement.*

Oven-bird

Pample—1. to walk lightly on tiptoe; 2. to fidget.

Pan—to press down or crush. Heavy vehicles may be said to "pan" agricultural land, making cultivation difficult.

Pangle—a badly-drained field.

Parish lantern—the moon.

Par-yard—bullock yard.

Pass/passe—temper.

Pattens—old Fenland name for skates, especially those with blades turned up in front.

Pawking—beachcombing or collecting sticks for kindling.

Paxwax—gristle in meat.

Pearks—gadgets, inventions - "I dunt hold wi'orl these modin pearks".

Ped—a basket (cf pedlar).

Peerking—looking for something, nosing around.

Pensy—fretful.

Perk—to perch. Also a rather irreverent nickname for the top of the rood screen in church.

Petman—smallest pig in the litter.

Petty—outdoor lavatory. Possibly from the French "petit" - small - the smallest room.

Pick-cheese—bluetit.

Pie-wipe—lapwing.

Pig—1. a woodlouse; 2. tapering course of bricks laid to correct levels, occasionally seen in old buildings.

Pightle—small field or enclosure.

Pingle—to toy with food (qv mank).

Pinpaunches—winkles.

Pipy—descriptive of a plant run to seed, shot.

Pishamire—ant. There are several variations.

Pishamire barneybee—earwig. (Combination of words for ant and ladybird.)

Pitcher—*man loading sheaves of corn on to wagon.*

Pivet—*privet.*

Plancher—*a wooden floor.*

Plantin'—*plantation of young trees.*

Plate—*the tyring platform at a smithy on which the heated iron tyre was positioned round a wooden wheel.*

Plawks—*hands.*

Plump—*bread soaked in hot water to which butter, sugar or dripping has been added.*

Pod—*belly.*

Poke-cart—*miller's cart for carrying "pokes" or sacks.*

Polly dishwasher—*pied wagtail (also Nanny dishwasher)*

Pollywiggle—*tadpole. Other versions include pot-ladle.*

Popple—*1. poplar tree; 2. nonsense.*

Potchet—*piece of broken pottery.*

Prating—*noise hens make after laying.*

Pricker bag—*farmworkers' dinner bag.*

Primmicky—*putting on airs, or finnicky.*

Pritch—*1. to prick; 2. eel-gaff with three prongs.*

Proper—*undoubted, obvious.*

Prugging about—*wandering about.*

Puckaterry—*muddle or confusion, distress (cf purgatory).*

Pudding-poke—*long-tailed tit, from the shape of its nest.*

Puet—*black-headed gull.*

Pug—*wash a few clothes through quickly, - "Just pug these through".*

Puke—*disagreeable person.*

Pulk/pulk-hole—*small pond or spring of water.*

Pummace/pommace—*pulp from apples used in cider-making.*

Push—*a boil or carbuncle.*

Putter—*to nag, mutter to oneself. ("u" as in nut)*

Putting on his parts—*misbehaving, trying to get his own way.*
Pwidge—*a puddle.*

Quackle/quaggle/squackle—*to choke or strangle - "This here new collar wholly fare ter quackle me!".*
Quant—*punt pole used on Broads or to use such a pole.*
Queer—*sick, out-of-sorts - "I dunt harf feel queer".*
Quick—*twitch or couch-grass.*

Rabbit—*in carpentry, to rebate or cut grooves.*
Rafty—*with reference to weather, damp, chilly and windy.*
Rainbird—*green woodpecker, its tapping considered a sign of rain.*
Rally—*shelf built into a wall.*
Randan—*second sifting of meal at the flour mill.*

Quick

Ranny—*a shrew mouse.*

Rare—*often used in connection with anything unusual or remarkable, as an adjective or adverb. Sometimes rendered as "rea'" - abbreviation of "real". - "Thass a rare ole muddle", and "He travel rare fast".*

Rather of the ratherest—*intoxicated.*

Rattick/rattock—*noise.*

Raw—*annoyed, angry. - "He wunt harf raw".*

Razor-grinder—*nightjar.*

Reasty—*rancid.*

Reed-pheasant—*bearded tit.*

Reel-a-bobbin—*cotton reel.*

Reemer—*1. an expert; 2. a heavy rain.*

Rhizzes—*hazel branches, formerly used in wattle and daub building.*

Riffle—*to break up the surface of a field by shallow cultivation.*

Rightside—*to beat a naughty child.*

Rigs—*space between furrows on ploughed land.*

Rimes—*a rime frost.*

Ring-dow—*ringdove or pigeon.*

Ringes—*lines or rows of trees or plants.*

Roaring boys—*men who salted herring.*

Roding—*clearing dykes.*

Roger/Roger's blast—*a small whirlwind, usually regarded as a sign of unsettled weather.*

Roke—*mist or fog. (rokey or roky)*

Roment—*1. rumour or tall story; 2. to spread a false report.*

Ronds—*marshy borders of a river.*

Room of/rume o'—*instead of, in place of - "I see he hev got greenhouse room of his garden shed what he took down".*

Rootling—*burrowing, rooting, usually connected with pigs.*

Rorping—*a loud noise as of a bull bellowing.*

Rorping

Roughing—*turning in the heels of horse-shoes to form calkins, or small spurs, to prevent the horse slipping in icy weather.*

Rows—*narrow streets of old Yarmouth, once numbering over a hundred.*

Rub—*stone for sharpening tools.*

Rubbidge—*rubbish or weeds.*

Ruck—*to crease.*

Rude—*rough, untidy or poorly done. Also descriptive of weather.*

Rum'un—*strange one - "Thass a rum'um". Also used to describe a bit of a lad - "He ent harf a rum'un!".*

Run—*to leak, with reference to kettles, watering cans etc.*

Run on—*to grumble or exaggerate - "he dunt harf run on!"*

Runnel—*a wheel.*

Runcie—*a cart horse.*

Sadly—*poorly, unwell.*

Sail-reaper—*horse-drawn harvester, with which up to ten acres of corn could be cut in a day.*

Sally/Sarah/Sukey—*a hare.*

Sammucking—*wandering, strolling aimlessly.*

Santer—*a stroll.*

Sase—*layer of large flints occurring in chalk.*

Sawney—*foolish, usually used in confessing to doing something silly - "Ent I an ole sawney!".*

Scald—*highest part of a field.*

Scalder—*a large number, a crowd.*

Scissor-grinder—*grasshopper warbler.*

Scores—*path down cliffs, or narrow streets leading to beach.*

Scoring/scoring up—*hoeing sugar beet after initial chopping out.*

Scorf—*to scoff.*

Scrab/scrorp—*to scratch.*

Screws—*rheumatic pains.*

Scrouging—*crowding together, crushing.*

Scud—*to shake herring out of the nets.*

Scuppit—*a scoop or ditching tool.*

Scutes—*projecting angles of an irregularly-shaped field, often presenting difficulty when ploughing.*

Seal/sele—*a time or season.*

Seam—*lard or dripping. "Bread and seam" once made many a meal.*

Sea-pie—*oyster catcher, from its pied plumage.*

Seat—*sitting, of eggs.*

Sed-lip—*container suspended from shoulders in front of the body for use when broadcasting seed or fertiliser.*

Seed-fiddle—*appliance for sowing, seed scattered from a container by means of a wheel turned by the action of a bow with a leather thong.*

Seft—*saved.*

Seggs—*rushes (from sedge).*

Several/savrul—*a considerable number, usually more than the word suggests. A crowd of 20,000 at Carrow Road draws the Norfolk response - "Savrul there!".*

Shack—*1. to wander around; 2. grain lying in the field after harvest; 3. to turn out animals or poultry on the harvested field to feed on any remaining grain.*

Shack-time—*period in autumn for gleaning or "shacking".*

Shammock—*a slovenly girl.*

Shannock—*native of Sheringham, and whose parents were both born in the town. Some insist grandparents as well.*

Shanny—*excited, wild, scatterbrained.*

Sharm—*to scream or shout.*

Shat—*shirt.*

Shay-brained—*silly.*

Sheers/shires—*counties outside East Anglia.*

Shoof

Shell-carr—*variety of carrstone used in West Norfolk buildings.*

Shet—*shut.*

Shig/shug—*to shake or wave about.*

Shim—*the blaze on a horse's face.*

Shiver—*small splinters of wood in the finger.*

Shock—*group of sheaves of corn in the harvest field.*

Shod—*past tense of shed, with reference to taking off clothing. - "He was that hot he shod his jacket".*

Shoof—*a sheaf of corn.*

Shot—*1. a young boar pig; 2. of plants run to seed.*

Shrog—*rough-coated or diseased rabbit or other animal.*

Shruck—*past tense of shriek - "She shruck wi'larfter".*

Shruff—*twigs and sticks for making a fire.*

Shuck—*the shell of peas, or to shell anything.*

Shucky/shuckety—*untidy, slovenly.*

Shud—*shed. "Shud down the yard" - outside toilet.*

Shufflewing—*hedge sparrow.*

Shuft—*to move or push along. (to shift)*

Shug—*to shake or scatter.*

Shutten Saturday—*day after Good Friday (Shut-in Saturday).*

Shutten-up-time —*getting dark.*

Sibbits—*banns of marriage (or sibrits).*

Sight—*a lot, a good deal - "I'm feelin'a sight better terday".*

Signify—*to matter, usually heard in the negative - "That dunt signify whether he come or not".*

Sillybold—*cheeky - "Dunt yew be so sillybold!".*

Sisserera—*a heavy blow.*

Skep—*big wicker basket.*

Skinker—*lad who fetched the beer at harvest time or filled the glasses and horns at ale-house parties.*

Skrowge—*crowd together, squeeze, push.*

Skep

Skriggle—*to squirm like an eel.*
Skunt—*skinned, of knees.*
Skywannicking—*fooling around.*
Slad—*flooded land.*
Slade—*a sledge.*
Slantendicular—*not quite perpendicular.*
Slarred—*daubed.*
Slarver—*1. to dribble (saliva), drool; 2. to talk rubbish - "He dew slarver on!".*
Slop—*1. a coarse drill material; 2. apron or working smock; 3. wet ground.*
Slop-footed—*walking with toes turned outwards.*
Slopping jacket—*loose fitting jacket with large pockets.*
Slub—*mud.*
Slummocking—*ungainly, clumsy - "A slummocking gret mawther".*
Sluss—*slush, mud, dirty water.*
Smeath/smea—*open area of low-lying land.*
Smee—*wild duck.*
Smittick/smittock—*very small piece.*

Smore—*to throng or crowd.*

Smoult—*to become calm (of the sea).*

Smur—*light rain or drizzle. Also used as a verb - "That ent rainin' much, only smurrin'".*

Snack—*door latch.*

Snaste—*long wick on a burning candle.*

Snasty—*bad-tempered.*

Sneerfroys—*supercilious.*

Snew—*snowed. (Hew -hoed; mew - mowed; shew - showed)*

Snob—*a shoemaker.*

Sole—*beat - "He dint harf give him a soling".*

Soler—*anything surprisingly large in size - "Thass a soler!".*

Soller—*a loft.*

Sorft—*silly - "He's as sorft as they cum!".*

Sosh—*"on the sosh" means not upright.*

Sow—*a woodlouse.*

Spantry—*threshold (also troshel).*

Spars—*rafters.*

Spawle—*1. to shout; 2.to spit out.*

Spink—*chaffinch.*

Splar/splaar—*to spread.*

Spolt/spoult—*brittle, crisp.*

Spong—*narrow strip of low-lying marshy ground.*

Spreed—*to spread - "Muck-spreedin' time".*

Sprit—*a quant or punt pole.*

Sprung—*split.*

Spud—*a weeding tool on a long handle or walking stick, also known as a dock-chisel or grubber.*

Spuffle—*to fuss or bustle about.*

Squat—*"keep it squat" means to treat something as secret*

Squinder—*to burn very faintly, like damp fuel which does not kindle into a flame.*

Squinny—*lean and lanky.*

Squit—*nonsense, light-hearted conversation, an unlikely story - "A load of ole squit!".*

Stag—*a cock turkey or a wren.*

Staithe—*landing stage.*

Stam—*to amaze or astonish.*

Stand up—*to shelter or wait under cover.*

Stank/stanch—*a dam.*

Stannickle—*a stickleback.*

Stark—*stiff or tight.*

Stew—*cloud of dust.*

Stewpe—*to drink noisily, possibly from stoup - a drinking vessel.*

Stewkey Blues—*cockles from Stiffkey.*

Stifler—*busy person, usually taking a lead. "Hid stifler" - head man or leader. Foreman on a farm.*

Stingy—*unkind, harsh (pronounced stinjy).*

Stive—*dust. To "kick up a stive" means to raise the dust, literally or figuratively.*

Stone house—*a stone beer bottle.*

Stoppages—*epileptic fits.*

Stover—*winter food for livestock on the farm.*

Strammacking—*travelling around.*

Strome—*to walk quickly with long strides.*

Strong-docked—*well-built, thick-set about the hips and thighs.*

Strupe/stroop—*throat.*

Stuggy—*stocky.*

Stulp—*a post of any kind.*

Sue—*to discharge (boil or wound).*

Suffin' goin' abowt—*Norfolk's most common ailment!*

Sukey—*a hare.*

Summer lamb—*the snipe (from its bleating call).*

Summer snipe—*sandpiper.*

Sunket—*snack or morsel of food.*

Suslams—*mixture of food, like trifle.*

Sustificate—*traditional corruption of "certificate".*

Swale—*shade.*

Swallacking—*very hot (swale-lacking?).*

Swarston winder—*a black eye. Could be connected with Swardeston or with Swart, meaning dark, i.e. a darkened window.*

Sways—*hazel rods used in thatching.*
Swede/swedebasher—*native of Norfolk.*
Swedge—*a blacksmith's hammer.*
Swidge—*a small puddle.*
Swift—*a newt.*
Swill—*basket containing 500 herring.*
Swimmers—*Norfolk dumplings.*
Swipe—*sickle.*
Swoddy—*soldier.*

Tack—*scythe handle.*
Tannup—*pocket watch on a chain (turnip)*
Teamer—*a teamer or team of horses consisted of five animals, two to work all morning, two all afternoon and one resting, resulting in one day off in five. Teaman - man in charge of horses.*
Tempest—*a thunderstorm, rather than a storm of rain and strong wind as defined in the dictionary.*
Ter—*the, that, this.- "Ter field look good ter year".*

Tetter/twiddle—*pimple.*
Tewk—*redshank.*
Thack—*1. to thrash or beat; 2. to thatch.*
Thapes—*gooseberries.*
That'll larn yer! —*serves you right!*
Thew—*thawed. Thow - to thaw.*
Thick-knee—*Norfolk plover or stone curlew.*
Thillers—*gear for cart, harness.*
Thongy—*close or oppressive weather.*
Thredickle—*unsettled.*
Tidiff—*bluetit.*
Tidy—*good or fair.*
Tiller—*to throw out many stems from a root.*
Time—*while - "I could ha' dun that job time he wuz yappin' bowt it".*
Tipe—*pit dug for trapping rabbits - an old Fenland word.*
T'is an' t'aint—*sow thistle - it is a thistle - and it isn't a thistle!*
Titchy—*irritable, touchy.*

Tit-faggots—*bundle of small sticks used for fuel.*

Tit-lark—*meadow pipit.*

Tittermatorter—*see-saw*

Tittle-me-fancy—*pansy*

Titty-totty—*very small.*

Tizzick—*troublesome cough.*

Tom-breezer—*dragon fly.*

Trave—*wooden frame in which lively colts were held for shoeing.*

Trav'us—*(trave house) - yard or open space near the village smithy.*

Tricolate—*to decorate or repair - "I'm gorter tricolate my ole shud"; also "tittivate".*

Trosh—*to thresh.*

Troshel—*threshold.*

Trow—*trough.*

Truck—*rubbish.*

Tudded—*(toaded) i.e. bewitched.*

Tumbler—*a tumbril.*

Twilting—*a beating.*

Twizzle—*to spin or twist.*

Tittermatorter

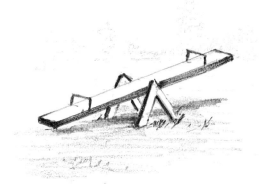

Unean—*underneath.*

Ungain—*awkward, inconvenient, clumsy.*

Uppards and downards—*colourful description of sickness and diarrohea*

Upright—*to live upright means to have sufficient income without having to work for a living.*

Useter—*used to - "I useter go ter the pictures".*

Vacajees—*wartime evacuees. (Also wacajees).*

Note: many words beginning with V take a W start in Norfolk - warmint, wittles and willage among them. There are also examples of the letter being changed in the middle of a word i.e. aggravating becomes aggraweartin'.

Waps/Wapsy—*wasp.*

Warmint—*varmint or vermin, troublesome person - "Come here yew young warmint, I'll sort yew out!".*

Wash'us—*wash house.*

Weesh/weesht—*command to horse to go to the right.*

Wennel—*a weaned calf.*

Weskut—*waistcoat.*

Wet-shed—*with wet feet - as opposed to dry-shod.*

Wheatsel—*time of wheat sowing.*

Whelm—*to empty bucket or other receptacle.*

Wherry—*distinctive Norfolk Broads sailing barge, with a single huge black sail.*

Whifflers—*attendants who cleared the way for Norwich Corporation processions on Guild Days.*

Whippletree—*drawbar to which horses' traces were attached on a plough or harrow.*

Wholly—*very, completely, used for emphasis - "That cake taste wholly good, bor!".*

Wibbled—*untidily packed.*

Wick—*nerves - "git on yer wick".*

Wherry

Wicket-hole—*purpose-built hatch between barn wall and building next door.*
Widdles—*1. pimples; 2. ducklings.*
Will-Jill—*woman of masculine appearance.*
Will-o-wix—*owl (also Billy-wix).*
Windle—*small skep without handles, made of fine and skinned willows.*
Winnick—*to whimper.*
Wire in—*to wire in means to eat ravenously.*
Without—*unless - "He wunt go without she go anorl".*
Wittery—*weak.*
Wittles—*food (victuals).*
Woodsprite—*woodpecker.*
Worrit—*to worry or annoy.*
Wry—*fault or mistake - "There ent a wry in'em" is praise!*
Wypers—*lapwings.*

Yallerified—*appearance of corn crop after a long cold and wet spell of weather.*
Yarm—*to eat greedily.*

Yarmandering—*talking at length, reminiscing.*

Yarmouth capon—*a red herring.*

Yelk—*yolk of an egg.*

Yellums—*bundles of reed for thatching. Yelming is combing thatch.*

Yelt—*a young sow.*

Yisty—*yesterday.*

Yoke—*to harness horses.*

Yorks/yorkers—*strings tied round labourer's trousers (qv 'Lijahs).*

Yourn—*yours.*

Yow—*to yell or chatter or howl. (To fretful child during a meal - "Evy time yew yow, yew lose a chow").*

Zackly—*exactly - "Thass zackly ryte!"*

Yellums

The Final Exam

A prestigious diploma in Norfolk Culture should be yours if you can get through this final passage inside five minutes without tripping up more than once.

Our multiple uses of the word "do" - or, as we pronounce it "dew" - are highlighted in this memorable item pieced together by Anthony Hammond several years ago. It still serves as a rigorous examination for those who claim to know their Norfolk. The scene is a country railway station where a mother is seeing her small boy off on holiday with his uncle. She says:

"Dew yew make him dew as yew dew: don't, he 'on't dew as he should dew. If he don't dew as he should dew, I should give him a dewin' tew if I was yew. We dew our tew. I always say tew'm, "Don't dew it, don't dew it, 'cause if yew dew that don't dew"; and neither dew it, dew it? So dew yew mind what he dew dew. I don't want he should go and dew anything like he done up at Mrs Dewin's, Tuesday. Mrs Dunne come out time he was a-dewin' of it, and when she see what he done to Mrs Dewin's dewins she say, "Oh! Whatever have yew done?" she say, and runned off to fetch Mrs Dewin'. That wouldn't ha' done, Mrs Dewin' say, for Mrs Dunne to a' done nothin tew the boy, dew I might ha' gone round, she say, and got aboard o' Mrs Dunne for nothin', not knowin', but Oh! what a t'dew when Mr Dewin' come back an' see Mrs Dunne gettin' all the dewins. "Hew done it?" he says. "Why, little Alfie," Mrs Dunne say, so he say, "Dew yew tell his mother from me, if he dew'ny more like that I'll dew him!" Old lady Dunne see him tew, but she was then arter some feathers for old deaffie Gotobed, and y'know what an old dardalum-dew he is, so that put har in a stew for a minute for fear the wind blew. Well, that was a how-d'ye-dew, I tell yew, and Mrs Dewin' then got all ready for Dunham's man to take 'em. Mrs Dunne say little Dewin' wouldn't never ha' done half what he done, but there y'are. Well, there y'go. Fare y'well."

So, how did yew dew?